Everyone I Love, Alive

Cover design by Kimberley Arteche

Interior design by Laura Joakimson
Interior typefaces: Optima and Joanna MT Std

Library of Congress Cataloging-in-Publication Data

Names: Bayani, Jason, author.
Title: Everyone I love, alive / Jason Bayani.
Description: Oakland, California : Omnidawn Publishing, 2025. | Summary:
"With this collection of poems, Jason Bayani leans into traditions of
lyric, song, and prayer to cultivate life while existing within a time
of empire and societal collapse. Everyone I Love, Alive wrestles with
form to summon both the living and the dead. Bayani's rich language
calls us to experience a connection to cultural heritage and, even
during times of oppression, to find the compassion and awareness needed
to drive change. These poems show how not only our love and desires-but
also our rage and resistance-can be the very things that keep us
alive"-- Provided by publisher.

Identifiers: LCCN 2025015624 | ISBN 9781632431684
(trade paperback ; acid-free paper)
Subjects: LCGFT: Poetry.
Classification: LCC PS3602.A984 E94 2025 | DDC 811/.6--dc23/eng/20250411
LC record available at https://lccn.loc.gov/2025015624

Published by Omnidawn Publishing, Oakland, California
www.omnidawn.com
10 9 8 7 6 5 4 3 2 1
ISBN: 978-1-63243-168-4

Reading Bayani's tender, searing collection is like bearing witness to a modern-day harana: a lover under the beloved's window, singing out from the heart. Only here the beloved is the world; the future; the possibility of liberation. Bayani's lucid, questing poems sing to these endangered things with a voice full of heartache, fury and hope—knowing too that a serenade, like any poem, is a way to share the breath of life. These poems do just that: they see that which is nearly lost, nearly gone and then they go to work—they resuscitate.
—Elaine Castillo, author of *America Is Not the Heart, How to Read Now* and *Moderation*

This is—dare I say—Jason Bayani's most mystical book, a mighty alchemy of prayer and fury that was, for me, an invitation to feel with the honesty of water. A loss beyond language pulses through these poems; in its wake, a homecoming to stillness that's deeply reparative and surprisingly thrilling. As always, Bayani is a tender witness to history's brutality and beauty, which feels like a call to (now more than ever) remain human. *Everyone I Love, Alive* is vintage Jason Bayani: loving, broken, broken open, capacious, searching, and shot through with an aching and "audacious light."
—Brynn Saito, author of *Under a Future Sky*

Jason Bayani's third book 'Everyone I love, Alive' is a triumph. The poems in this collection vibrate with the urgency of a dying world inviting the reader into a living present. This book holds cities, mythology, and memory. This book is brimming with questions that tear at the very fabric of our knowing and asks us to still love the world. If you're new to the Jason Bayani Fandom this is the perfect place to start, welcome.
—Sam Sax, author of *Yr Dead* and *Pig*

Everyone I Love, Alive

Jason Bayani

OMNIDAWN PUBLISHING
OAKLAND, CALIFORNIA
2025

Contents

I was born and I live as a believer, weary of vertigo

I say Bathala, Bathala, Bathala

as certain as the word creation does also mean
to begin.

Mixtape
Love Endeavor / Alice Smith (2006)

There is a voice in me, both
of water and fire. I write towards
what I am not in my life, outward and effusive,
a provocation. Help me document a history
of the living, everything
is urgent. The story is my love language.

Oh, baby, this love endeavor
Don't have to last forever
Come on and share
Whatever you want with me

When I slow down I release into everything
laid before me; the past which pulls me to witness.
I'm trying to open the door to another thought,
within the stretch I am made to listen.
I am looking for one beautiful breath in, one beautiful breath out.
How are we to know
what comes next? I will this body to
brave reception. I am the archive of you
as you are of me.

Oh, baby, this love endeavor
Don't have to last forever
Come on and share
Whatever you want with me

Life is only brief in retrospect.
Everything is long, everyone

is a universe, but we are not
forever and why should we be?
I will belong to the water in the end.
As will all I've written.

Someday, Again

I'm waiting for the words   to catch up to my heart
      which is elliptical at the moment   there's an apology

even I am expecting to barrel out of my throat

                  but what for
                  what for

I am continuing to write in a font   that displeasures
me
      everything shifts so rapidly

my body   the environment

                my body
                  the environment

why not return to something as aggressively unspectacular
      as Arial

a font for all my first thoughts   today I typed the words
              "someday, again"

and deleted and retyped   deleted and retyped

inside of the collapse   I am still holding on to narrative
this is not sentiment   it is how I keep my family together
when I breathe in deep enough I feel it   all the old anger
waiting to become newer anger   not having the words

can feel like not having something to hit

    I think I wrote that in another poem before

what is the equation that solves everything

                                ideas are commodity
      even the idea that ideas are commodity
        I don't even know
what I have to sell

                I've spent my entire life living on a fault line

    I know all that's been made is inherently broken.

This is not me being dour   this is me writing a note
that says I miss you   I meant that the other way
    (within space   or without)
but the one you were thinking works too

Between Time and Water

in all of the night and charitable smoke
water bristling on this skin and the fire
crackling in summer rain

tiny ruptures

there are eyes in the trees

Marcelo says don't whistle in the woods   you don't know
who will answer

though I never want to be a disturbance

especially in a place of rightful quiet

there has to be more

silence out there

I am asking for a memory to return

any memory that stems the remaking of me

thought collapses me   in the middle

I am small in this world   today   I am of little sound

that's all right   I think   perhaps there's another world where I
am a big noise

but here
quiet finds me in all places

Prayer

dear hands
dear severance
dear safety
dear deliverance
dear multitudes
dear liberation
dear madness
dear _____
dear healing
dear restitution
dear suffering
dear labor
dear persistence
dear rest
dear revival
dear desire
dear ceasefire
dear return
dear dream
dear climate
dear land
dear living
dear god
dear god
dear god

there is a place of language and movement
where I ain't losing myself
so much   maybe
I'll find the place where I don't lose anyone

else   there is no shape to memory   it is a weaver's grid.
the sound of palm fronds ripping across the vein

my grandmother threading a lattice to tell the life of her
through the slippage   everything down to our atoms is woven
maybe there is only the pattern of me left to discover

I have to believe
that this will solve it all
that this will accept
the labor of my hands

sometimes I catch myself lacing my fingers together
and the words remember me   sometimes a prayer
is just how we discover

our breath   and I'm trying to breathe these days
and these days are slipping through the sieve
of me   and I can't do anything else but count
the losses

there's any number of uses for the human heart
                                            it drives the blood
through the body   the blood that knows every part of you
my blood knows me better than I know myself.

what a strange machine I'm living in   made to need
more than I'm able to handle   maybe there is a name

for everything inside of me I have failed
                                        at giving form to
some undiscovered matter
that lives inside the absences
of us   there is an order to me   that is how
the universe works

Even I have a place
among the ones I make
and those that are made for me

noise is a sort of capture silence   undoing silence
     too little   in too much of a space

here will come   an odd comfort

     so many fists pounding
               at the same still body of water

there is something   that wants to get out

                    I hold my name

there is something that wants   and I

         want it back   the roots of me

            shudder

I bray at the concrete   whisper

into the cracks   I hold

my name   slap the spill off my palms   how we

gonna be strong enough for this

        who am I here   locked inside

the very breath of my name   a locus

    of release   there is a flaw

a place where it breaks.

     I'm starting to notch every day I haven't cracked

every day I pull the harmonics out of this fucked up noise

    I ain't gone   yet   there is a sound

I'm slapping my belly to keep time

                    my skin

          breaks

at the bend

               it snaps

          and I'm awake in a warm bed

it snaps

                    and I'm screaming loud enough

                         to be pulled from erasure

I do have a song   a trajectory
    all that memory has to give   healing is a circle widening
          a mapped place   the road
comes reckoning   all of our wild selves   reveling

your many hands   forging   the wheel
is not broken   yet   help me find my north   through there is
the unclaimed world   it is not unmovable

what if   we belonged to each other

                          all our gardens

           awakening

                          we   creatures of variable light

all I want is   to make each other visible

                    in this language where I find no center

                    so I make a field

           old growth and an armor of trees

                          an offered plate after visiting

the portals that come through you

                                                    if only

to see your breath as you see my breath

                          like a soft hum

                    inside of a thimble

what have you
forgiven
or been made
to forgive

there
in the foreground
or what was
behind it

such a particular
madness to love
what has been
killing you

or that this is
what the world
would have
to offer you
as survival

the city trees
keep falling
because they
are cutting
the roots
too close
to the base

what is living
today
but an endless
documentation
of lost things

aren't you
tired of it
in all your
notebooks
and photo galleries
and emails and
social media

I was looking
at the water
and it escaped
me
time or memory
the parabola
extending

whenever I am
losing myself
I am always told
the same thing
to find
where my feet
are touching
the ground

to draw
my breath
in
to draw
it back
out

I would
dream you
a place
of continuous
healing
one with
a quiet
hum

how beautiful
the sound of
your breathing
how much
of awe
inside of
your still

I have a belief

an image my mind
        tries to form itself around

to wear the land like memory
        to come alive in the soil

what is it to receive life in all this loss
to see

this cycle breaking
        this greater work
        this greater prayer

oh   this will hurt

and I will always   turn towards the hurt

let this be our becoming

as long as the sun
        as long as the sun

Fragments

What a time to be

    some light disaster
                yet the weight   too much
      and there

a frequency   skip to the chapter

on giving

      this should not be

                        see these

these hands   these fingers   the ridges

the way they shape an   m
means   good fortune

Maybe life is best seen in retrospect
      all its blessings
         there's enough
            enough to be made a revision

30 years ago there is a child holding a knife to his wrists
      but he's alive   now
          isn't this fortune manifest

it's dangerous to want   isn't it
      you want in the wrong place   the wrong time

your wanting comes within the space of the wrong people
        you declare a want that will be subsumed by other wants

what do you want to be
a body anchored to its own heart
nothing here connects right   they talk about it
like it's half in and half out   but really

it feels like being splayed into five different directions
all of want   ~~all of wanting~~
a footpath   a voice on the other end
clearer and clearer still
      saying
                      come

Elegy

at the end of speed is a perfect still
        maybe   then   death is a truer
state of motion   what I can say is   then   you are not gone
        from me   you have only
                    moved beyond my sight

would   then   memory be a slowing
                for what moves beyond time   to return
back to time

when we were young
                driving down the freeway at midnight

        the car stereo broken   so someone had to hold

the boom box in their lap

we had nowhere to go
        in this time before the weight of remembering
                the city lights on our faces   flickering

Ghost Story

I've shuttered too much of myself off
    to see them
when they come
who will need them most
         I have
endings to us   it makes for some
    spaces of lingering regret
where will be the coda
    there is a strangeness
it will consume you
they still live in the same room
    because they do

I'm afraid
I believe
    it is to the ones
      the only evidence
suggest lonely
difficulties
    and so
to our wandering
in the world
so we say
they slept
as they live

        everywhere

I am not a pragmatist every day. Often I have to fight
the cynic in me   to keep everyone I love

            alive

I make nothing

Ever the odd silence finds interruption   all of living
pockmarked by disruption   there is no fixed location
    where I am is the wound unstitching

again   I am asked
    how do you practice self care

        and I hesitate before saying
                I took it
    my space
of quiet

        sometimes healing requires
        a bit of violence

                I grapple
with that meaning   as if my whole self requires
the parts that must spend their time justifying
        the other parts

why do I apologize for what has been taken from me
why is living for too many a process of dying

        who were any of us before the trauma happened?

the world is so intensely large and unmanageable

        and aren't I the world

    too

and worlds aren't only conquered
                            they're monetized
                                    and what am I, then
who interrupts the sacred
who takes the hands that tend the Earth
                                    the patterns fall away and they must

what does your imagination demand   in reflection

today what I will make is nothing
                            I make nothing and I give it to you

all this nothing to occupy no location in your space

        measure to nil   heavier than it should be

Table Properties

A.1

mother is a moon		
	refracting	
		there is not enough light
my palms flat and heavy		a muddled and obvious tone
	in collapse	
the church in my throat		base metal
	there is no softer way forward	
waking is its own misdirection		
	here in repetition	
the worst of these memories		knocking against my shoulder
	I begin	thought with pulse

A.2

one track	is playing	track two is right here	
the	tempo		is the same
after this	phrase		is done
I'm going to start		my transition	here

one track		is two track	the same
the	tempo		is right here
after my transition	is done		
I'm going to start		this phrase	here

the tempo	is done	my transition	
the same			one track
I'm going to start		after track	
this phrase			here

A.3

there is a river		
	refracting	
		find me in its tributary
some myth of return		
		and so I begin
	in collapse	
I am not sorry today		I have none to offer
	there is no softer way forward	
time escapes me again		
	here in repetition	
all of my laughter		trembling inside my fist
	I begin	
		I begin again

40

Mixtape
Float (Coco & Breezy Remix) / Janelle Monáe (2023)

You have to wring it out
what wants to be spoken into
the room. On one side is
the resilience. A soft sharing
the profoundly unique parts
of our living, corporeal hungers.

I don't step, I don't walk,
I don't dance, I just float

How long have I been breathing incorrectly
a head apart from the body, our lives where
our bodies lie. To know pain is a certain wisdom
but I am getting tired of all this learning.
I only need just a minute to become something
less tangible; to be away from the world
in order to find my way back inside of it.

I don't step, I don't walk,
I don't dance, I just float

Everything transforms in the end, doesn't it? I'm waiting
to meet my healed self. He makes sure I'm steady.
He makes sure I don't have to walk around here, alone.

Mezzanine

I wanted to be able to tell you the story would be what saves us.
Because I believe we tell it better. Because we do. Because we build
better worlds. But the world is.

I'm sorry I thought I could give you something more hopeful. I
do have a lot of it, hope. The minutiae of living requires so much
of it. The first cup of coffee in the morning, work emails, grocery
shopping. I had to spend a little bit of hope on comfortable running
shoes, water, medicinal goods. Doing the laundry is a hopeful task,
isn't it? What is left for dreaming?

I want to be a living thing, I do. I am in possession of a body and
this body bounds into space and I impede space as any structure does
and I shape, too, and I am made and make and move through time in
gentle cuts.

I, too, am among you, searching for light. I know it is there. I haven't
yet learned how to feel for it.

How does one feel light? By an increase in temperature, a prickly
sensation in your fingertips, am I focusing too much on my hands?
Do you feel light in the softest part of your throat?

What is it that called you to today? Can you ask it to call me, too.

I dream of a world and the world always escapes me. A softer place of
landing which cities are not.

I still believe we will win, but my god this world is doing a shit job
of backing me up.

42

I wanted to be able to say the story was never meant to be a method of containment, but I know this is wrong. Stories were told to maintain order. Stories were made to control. Stories can be such terrible, terrible things.

But I will tell a story of location. The place where your feet touch the ground, a footstep that emits light, how we take space with unending depths of nerve.

The Depths

I.

There is a rupture. A feeling. Always. There. Inside. I'm waving my
hand around in theoretical space like a dumbass trying to look for it.
This thing I'm trying to share with you.

In Tagalog there is a word, hugot, which means to pull out; however,
it's never used as a verb. Hugot only is.

Hugot shares the same nebulous space as "deep"— you know how
when you say deep and you mean profound but I'm not really trying
to think too hard about it. You say something is deep because you're
pointing to where it is resonating. An unmapped place. So maybe it is
not pulled: it is drawn, it is beckoned, or maybe it just erupts.

My theory of the self posits an inner world that lives in a separate
dimensional space. We are bigger on the inside. Wink.

If hugot is and hugot is of, then there must be a where. Hugot is not
hugot by merit of feeling or emotion, it must be labored towards, it
must be earned.

Hugot is often placed under a romantic context. In Philippine cinema
it is the outward expression of want, longing, pain— in this it is the
antithesis to Wong Kar-Wai's repressed eroticism, which doesn't make
it any more honest, it just makes it more vocal.

My cousin is a director in the Philippines. He specializes in romantic
dramas, the kind where the trailers feature light skinned actors
with delicate features crying at each other in taglish under a soft-
focus lens. In his films love is gained, love is lost, and we are always

struggling to understand where our love must go. In the desperation and passions is where everyone will point to where the hugot is, but I see the way he holds the male body in his frame. It is gentle and reverent and horny as fuck.

II.

Hugot is not a verb, but it is an action, it is a noun in motion. At times I hear someone say that something has hugot, but can hugot be possessed?

Is it an object from the depths or is it the depths itself? And we pull it to the surface, we pull it into language, and from language to voice, from voice to blood and body. Is hugot offered? Or can it only arrive the way that lightning trees in the sky as if to fill a form already lain there.

Can I say the hugot is my own? Is the depths an individual or communal space? And if my hugot is your hugot, what could we be, then?

III.

In the Philippines, every goodbye we make in this country will sound like the one I overhear my aunt tell my mother before we leave the family reunion in Butuan City. Through tears she says, I don't want to leave yet, but I have to.

This is the refrain, this is the music of departure. Always having to go, never wanting to. Knowing "here" is only temporary and "there" is always the distance between.

My father, the last child of ten, has lost almost all of his brothers. There is only his oldest, who is bedridden and stays in the downstairs floor of my cousin's townhome. When we visit my dad wakes him up and for a few minutes he stares at my father's face until he finally utters his childhood nickname, Tikboy. He says it again to assure himself, Tikboy, touching my father's face, and there the years fold into themselves briefly, all the years of being collapsing into this moment. Memory, which resists form. I will posit, then, hugot also transcends time.

My uncle turns to me and says, aren't you the poet? He says, I know a poem and begins to recite Jose Rizal's Mi Ultimo Adios.

> *Adios, Patria adorada, region del sol querida,*

Often when an elder says bye to me here, they also say, I won't see you, again,

> *Perla del Mar de Oriente, nuestro perdido Eden!*

and I know this is him saying there isn't time left

> *A darte voy alegre la triste mustia vida,*

49

and I say hugot is life within all of the losing

> Y fuera más brillante más fresca, más florida,
> Tambien por tí la diera, la diera por tu bien.

and I still don't believe hugot is something that can be owned,
but I do believe it can be given.

IV.

I can't stop thinking of migration in all its forms, of borders— who has access to move freely, why we move, what we leave behind, who gets to define them, who is left to reconcile with it all.

What is the particular grief of movement? I left home once and came running back two years later with an ache I still can't reconcile, but I know the other side as well, that when you're away, you're away, and you learn to be a person who is there, to make a home of there, and there is a place you will always have to convince yourself is here.

Maybe in America this is why we were drawn first to jazz, then R&B, disco, and hip-hop. The soul of soul music drawn from a depth. Online I swipe up on a video of three Filipino boys singing Beyoncé's "Listen" on some variety show, each taking turns trying to outbelt the other, slapping a little extra on what they can remember of each of her flourishes. It is a significant amount of mimicry, the intense stares, hand movements crashing downwards to punctuate each note— but is it soul? The same soul that when you hear it said out the right mouth feels like it's whipping around the stomach until it echoes into the infinite. What in America has allowed us to access hugot more than Black art forms? In soul, hugot sees kin.

It is said that with hugot what is drawn out is never violent or hateful. There can be anger, there can be frustration, and I will offer rage, as well. But the depth it accesses, though it may not be the seat of love, it is loving, it is care, it is wonder, it is hugot, and if there is hugot, is there also a place that does not abide by hugot's rules?

V.

On long drives I've made a habit of filming out the window. I
just want to remember it all, the rush of palm leaves, how the
roads cleave into towns and all the storefronts and people walking
alongside, all of it appearing so precariously close to the lens. I don't
want this to be some blur of a memory like all my memory of this
place has been. Whenever I was asked what this country was like,
I'd have the same answer, it was hot and it was green, a green unlike
anything I had ever seen before.

My cousin drives me around the city, we pull to the side of the road
and pick bayabas from the car windows, he plays their version of
good street/bad street, takes a photo of me flipping off the Magellan
statue.

I don't bring up the president. I know how popular he is in this
province and, forgive me, I just wanted to have my family back for
the few days I was here.

Up ahead I see an aspin walking across the street and make a joke
about how reckless all the dogs are out here. On this road any sudden
movements could send your car into one of the stalls or someone's
vehicle or into one of the pedestrians walking down the road. He
says, sometimes it's just safer to run over the dog than avoid it. As
we get closer it suddenly lays down in the middle of the street, my
cousin goes quiet, and I can see a tight purse of his lower lip before
he swerves the car around it.

VI.

When I arrive in the Philippines, over 5500 people have been
murdered in the president's drug war. And someone says, people are
dying everywhere. Someone says, there's such a thing as acceptable
dead. Someone says, they are not part of a useful and productive
society. Someone says, they will see we're only trying to liberate them
if you just let us kill them enough. Someone says, it is sad it is so so
sad, but...

If hugot is, then hugot must have something it is not. Should we say
it is another depth or does the opposite mean there is no depth to it.
Does it live in immediacy, the constant interruption of still.

Is it antithetical to life?

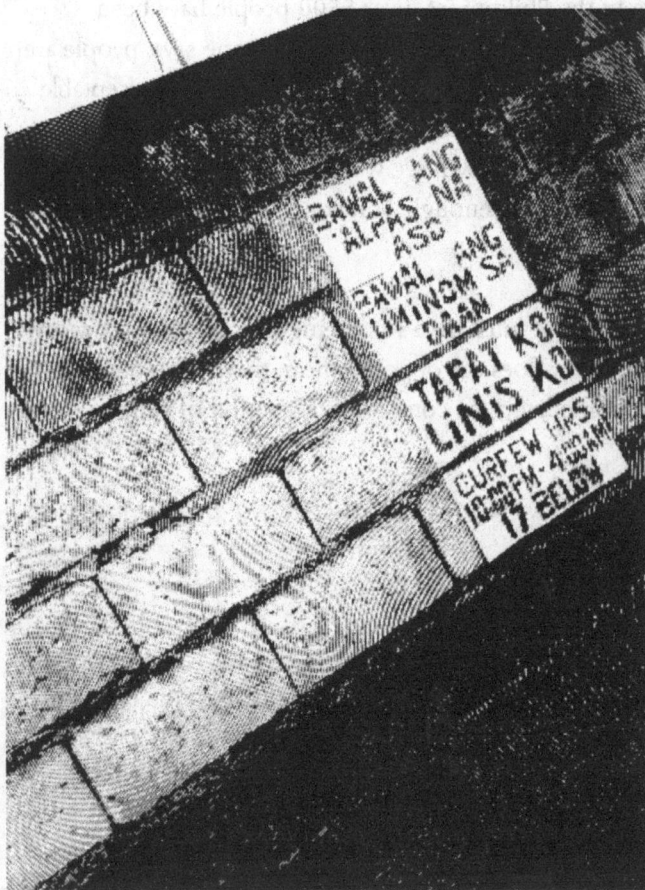

VII.

There is no pervasive madness anywhere, only desperation. And you
see it, too. The imbalance. All of abundance sacrificed to lesser gods.

Are you present right now? Are you? Where is your rage? Have you
held it sacred in all your quiet places. Do you have a quiet place left?
Or has it been quietly monetized for passive income and a little bit of
ad space?

Who holds your thoughts, your passions, all your wild dreaming?
I believe it belongs to the depths, I do, but where does it belong to
now?

In DC comics, anti-life is an equation of transcendental math. It can
be obtained, held, and used to subjugate.

The villain, Darkseid is written with an obsession for the anti-life
equation. When he attains it, he overwrites the formula so that the
calculation always ends up at him.

There is a place where hugot is and a place where it is not. And the
place where it is I believe is a place where we feed each other, and
the place where it isn't— who does it feed?

VIII.

What is it to be a person who doesn't dream? Who is consumed only by what they have and what they can't have. By what are they beheld?

The expanse narrows in the immediate. I write towards what I struggle to believe. I'm sorry, I spent too much time learning how to become a world that is comfortable with failure.

I'm afraid I've left too much of my hope online. Just let AI learn from it. It can generate more hope with fucked up looking hands.

I'm trying to imagine a river. Sometimes you start with a river because there's always a where beyond which the river runs through. It is and it is more, and right there is a path.

There in the depths I am still alone, but I am not apart. I need us to not be apart.

In the depths I hear you say, imagine a home, and there is a home.

In the depths, all my dead come alive, again.

In the depths, we pull and we pull

until we speak such audacious light.

The Wheel Is

How much of history is a man in a room
looking at a map saying, I want that. Nevermind
that a map is only an approximation of a space,

how we feed the imagination of borders, how we say
who gets to make a border. Maybe a country is nothing more
than a system of beliefs shaped by violent acts,

a creation myth that begins in death and is supplemented
with bibles

like the inhabitants of 7,641 islands suddenly finding themselves
countrymen. Because someone wanted,
wanted and believed they should have. As if
we were devoid of want, ourselves. As if certain wants
are to be subsumed by other wants. The violence
of our crafting flattens over the lens of time. And so we are,

but we are also in response to. That is the historic for us:
made against, moved within, moved through, moved in spite of—

so much of history is a document of people taking things from
other people.

There are books filled with them. The great takers of the world.
Movies where the taking is reimagined, but this time
everyone has really great abs.

A map started simply enough, right? Someone sitting in a room
wanting to know "where am I". I feel that so much.
I want to know where I am all the time.

When my parents looked at a map
they saw that to want would mean to lose.
To have would mean to lose. That our desires
are wrapped in cost.

Once a man told me he wanted to pray for my happiness.
and wouldn't I join him in praying for us all to be happy.

I don't wish to pray for anyone's happiness.
Happiness is passive.

I pray for your liberation. May all beings be free.
I can get happiness with a chocolate chip cookie.

I want time. I will take it. Even if it is spent and used up,
and written and written over again. Even with it burdened
and renamed. Even if it was made to wear
different clothes, a different tongue.

Even if it speaks the wrong language, even if I have to speak
the wrong language back.

I want this very history to fold back into itself. I want it to know
my damn name.

A clock ain't nothing but a series of gears. Time is a machine.
I'm pretty good at breaking machines.

Mixtape
Summertime Summertime / Nocera (1987)

Alixa asks, how many harvests do we have left?
Everything this land has given to us,
what do we have to give back?
There is an access point
a temple made of water
it becomes clearer and clearer still

take me
take me to the water
summertime, summertime

she says we can make a song, a ruckus
the magnetic field produced by the heart
there within, my being to become
she says something is dying while something else
is desperately trying to be born
I imagine the stone that bears fruit
a we beyond the physical body
like a simple cloth between us

take me
take me to the water
summertime, summertime

let it be the first words that come to your mind
welcome back to the way ahead
this must begin with the will to falter.

Fracture

Typhoons are massive things,
but so are countries. On a map
it can look like a bullet bearing through it.
And when a bullet pierces through
it ruptures everything around it.
So many branches of fracture
building off of one line. The body
is a bold and brilliant structure
but it breaks at the same scale it is built.
My friend says she can't keep living
in the same house anymore
listening to the sound of gunshots
waking her up in the morning.
And we keep drawing lines on maps
trying to determine the trajectory
of destructive forces. But here I am
telling a story of how I was ten years old
and took the worst hit in my life
when another kid kicked me flush on the face.
But I never said once that my face hurt,
because everything hurt, and everything hurt
after. I am always scoffing at the notion
of how a butterfly's wings can build into
a typhoon halfway across the world.
As if violence can have such a docile beginning,
As if we weren't made of bullets ourselves or the triggers.
Or everything that is caught in the breaking.

Basilisk

Pressure is an element derived
of itself. Even after its release
enough remains to hold the newer
form. I am told that I must release
everything that doesn't serve me.
This is the principle I am asked to
bend myself towards. Even stretching
is painful these days. All this pressure,
they say, stifles the blood. It's how
the heart fails you, forced to push
through a system that moves like mud.
At some point you can't just release
the pressure but what pressure has made
of you. I can't help but think of the luxury
in this. There is no country for tenderness.
How do you preserve this in others,
and ask them to survive the cities
that are made in opposition to them?
I believe there is a greater strength
in openness, the ability to allow feeling
to move through the body. But this is
a quiet religion amidst so much
righteous noise. They're always looking
for people like me. Living like some kind
of low-toned hum they can't stop hearing
and need to snuff out. This is how a body
turns to stone. And you say, this might
kill me later, but we're out here now.
We're trying to survive, now.

Survival is not a meritorious endeavor it is what happens in the margins

What do I have to account for? That I could leave a space
before my legs do, or that I know how it is done? And, yet,
this here is the ache to which I am always returning.

Everything is going to shit in this world. In the city
it is shit. In the state it is shit. In the country, shit.
The world, shit. The universe is vast and empty
and even more vast and more empty and apparently
even black holes can collide against each other
and send out ripples of energy and matter that branch
and expand through all of that nothingness
like a series of tubes. Like it's the intestines
of the universe pushing along even more
shit. I finally love my day job. Nobody loves
their day job. This is why everything else is terrible.

I know the things my brain does to make the body
want to survive. It watches the man in the hang glider above us
and says, You are afraid of this. And the brain says
You are afraid because you want to live. And then
you remember that you want to live. This is why
when I am lost, I think of hang gliders.

I often want to be as good as people believe I am.
A lot of days, I win. Every other day I'm trying
not to lose. And here I am on a day where
even my own name escapes me and I think,
memory must be a thing that's earned,
even the momentary lapses.

So today I make a list. Of everything
I have fought to remember, the goodness
of people, the many uses of the human heart,
location and setting, that everything
isn't terrible. Not everything. Not the entirety
of it all.

Mixtape
You Can't Hide From Yourself / Teddy Pendergrass (1977)

How much trouble comes from men who lack
fluency in the language of their desires.
The way they crash into everything. All this yearning
and impulse, all this want crowding the space.
There's an intimacy to being punched in the face
You choke a little. It leaves you breathless.

you can lie all you wanna
but one day you're gonna
gonna breakdown
breakdown and let it all out

Someone with a podcast is saying this is what happens
to men who were once warriors— who aren't allowed
to be warriors, anymore. Which is so much sadder
than saying I hate being alone so much I'll fight anyone
for even the slightest moment of connection.
This is the best we could do, instead of engineering
a power that could be shared freely, we could only
devise a structure of it.

you can lie all you wanna
but one day you're gonna
gonna breakdown
breakdown and let it all out

What is worthy of our fight? Our rage? I am waiting
for who brings the light. There has to be somewhere
to put all of this, it must have somewhere to go.

Brutal Engine

We are inside an imbalance. Feel free to adjust this curriculum of unmaking. The colonial project is not over. Let this be a place of reweaving.

A thousand clay jars for all this grief. I make for you a place of landing, of storage. A living archive.
Say it.   I'm writing us back into history.

Say it.

Our homes will be our homes   again. We say land is life. Which is why, when they come for us, they come for the land as well.

Why do I apologize for what has been taken from me? In the spaces of omission, I find a truer you that finds a truer me. A still that revises the fracture. The only true evil in this world is the imposition of power. There are no complexities within. It is   at its core   a surrender. A god of consumption.

Who do you pray to? Creator   or destroyer.

Which of the god's faces mirrors your own?

What lives at the removal of abstraction, one that remembers our movement in the world as holy and processional rather than the result of empire and all its unending fires. If time is a myriad of forms then we are in the Brutal Engine, a history marked by what has been destroyed and what has been taken. Once we were the water and all of its possibilities, an ocean that rendered us bordered and, yet, borderless unfettered by the boat, which is the extension of our soul

the only worthy navigator of the unknown

We start off in life with conditioning, so we may be inured. What is the devil but that which separates you from the norm? I am a presence and a wound here.

A home of enduring regret.

Who has agency in this place? Who among us must carefully navigate it for a semblance of safety. So many of us make homes in countries that have killed us dispassionately.

We are the ones who are the bearers of your peace. We are the ones who maintain the order.

For the killing of a noncombatant to become justified, the opposition must demonstrate "irregularity", which denotes a rejection of form, a lack of adherence to. There is a civil way for you to die— which is to submit, which is to surrender, which is to acknowledge a greater power. Your hospitals, your schools, your places of worship, your homes— all your places of retreat and safety are muddled by irregularity. And inside

the irregularity persists newer and newer forms.

Civil warfare demands a certain purity.

And what greater purifier is there than the fire, and what greater bearer of fire in our hands is the bomb.

There is a light   somewhere, maybe in the red marrow of my bones. All of the news broke apart in my hands, yesterday. There are few horrors like those of a benevolent country.

The man on the TV says the only thing that matters

                     is us

In every other country I am "us", and here, I am until you say I'm not. But there is a light somewhere isn't there? Or do I have to break apart me just to find it? What will become of the restlessness in my blood. The sharp tingle in my palms that curls all of my fingers into fists.

We were not imagining a different world, we were too busy trying to keep afloat, too busy trying to survive this one. And here we were struggling to figure out how to survive a new landscape, and in this we learned,

or rather re-learned, how to imagine our worlds differently, alive with renewed imagination.

We can take their monuments,
     we can burn it down,
          we can build it back up.

We believed. We believed.

Every gain accumulates a debt. They will make you pay. Oh, they will make you pay.

Balance is unprofitable.

They will break you from your center and then offer you a weekend seminar on how to get back to it. And then they'll tell you how much progress you've made and just think about how much more progress you'll continue to make if you take our six-week course. And during the six-week course you'll learn there isn't just a center to you, but levels, and right now you are on level 5 and where you want to be is level 1— find out how with more classes, and more seminars, and one on one meetings with level 2s where you'll reveal, or in some cases, enact, all your most blackmailable secrets, because complete surrender of your ego and the offering of your vulnerability to a higher power is the only thing that will eliminate the angry microscopic aliens that live in your bloodstream and are the real reason why you can no longer find any true balance in this world,

which is what you find out at level 3.

I am only trying to live   as I know you are   too   amongst all this certainty   so much belief without
imagination   what is a god but a maker of things and to believe in a god   shouldn't that also mean a
belief in endless possibility.

Concession is such an unholy land.

Who taught us how to extract the self?   Who turned our gods into our monsters?
                                            The beast is the imbalance   it eats us out of time.

Where is my place   anymore
where is the red of me   where is a home

        for all this fury?

This is the thing about courage, I've known too many men who think they've found it the moment they see everything has been broken. Most people fight sloppy. Every punch wants to be a knockout. Every punch ain't ready for how much it will hurt.

We walk away angrier. It doesn't leave you. People only get tired of fighting what they can't win. You can't punch an idea or a country, there's just people. Why build when it can just as easily be broken? Why build when that isn't what anyone expects of you anyway? The fight isn't this, you know.

It isn't the cuts or all the bruising you won't feel until the next day. All that is just a wreckage. It is a ruin these hands of mine will make. I know enough people who will throw down with me, it doesn't take much—

but those who build and stay building, those who make (in spite of it all)

that is the only fight, the only brave I can manage anymore.

There in the absences are beginnings.   The form of it comes together
                                                        if I hold it long enough.

Such a staggering motion to the world, and, yet, we remain so stubbornly unmoved.

I am of a rational mind.

No one saves the world, but we can try to keep each other alive:
                                        within life instead of within dying.

Who deserves our praise more than the ones we choose to dance alongside?

In my hands will be the cup that holds all your laughter.

Beautification Project

Every city will become a ghost inside of itself.
We no longer wait for God to bring it to bone.
When the man guts the building, the temple is silent.
Each bit of scrap is a quell to hunger.
This is how we learn to eat metal.

Mixtape
Uptown / The Crystals (1962)

To build the Wall of Sound, Phil Spector
would run the musicians for as long as it took
to bleed the individual out until it blended all together.
Until it bled away error, the messiness of people,
their tired voices straining towards repetition.
To desire purity, is to desire power.

he gets up each morning and he goes downtown
where everyone's his boss
and he's lost
in an angry land

What kind of person looks at the voice in song,
this container of wants and longings, and imagines a wall?
The echo chamber was never meant to make
the sound acceptable. They were only for enhancement.
A right noise amongst so much intolerable noise.
There is always a little man. History won't stop
giving them to us. It won't stop asking us
to hold their anger as sacrosanct.

he gets up each morning and he goes downtown
where everyone's his boss
and he's lost
in an angry land

4/4 time in western culture is a method of containment.
How do you engulf a room from the inside of a machine?
This is the question, and you work backwards from it.

In Jerusalem

there is a break in the wall where a DJ climbs up a dingy ladder so
he can get to a gig he's booked in occupied territory   he's been
caught by the police a few times, already, but, as he says, he won't
stop   he's bringing music back to the place his family was
removed from years ago

every great act of resistance is built by smaller acts, and therein are
smaller acts

displacement is an excision from the body, one of the oldest
violences   there is an assumption that a wall is built for
protection, but a wall inflicts, it disrupts a people's belief in
belonging to a land   the wall appears in endless forms   there
are many ways to inure a people into seeing a home as something
they are meant to lose

sometimes what we are doing is rooting each other back into
Earth   to help   each other back to our bodies   the 4/4
drum pattern that gave birth to dance music is often called the
heartbeat   the way it centers repetition makes it akin to mantra
or prayer   to be together is to remember we exist

to be within is to find the will   we will give
life to each other this way   we will return
each other to ourselves   we will remember
those, too, who brought bread, or flowers, or song

the world will always bend to this   I must believe this is true
to us   they will listen

The Great City

a city is never abandoned
    just bled of its usefulness

the money made in development and never
the sustainability of life

great cities tell the story of great empires   the great cities
of this world   grind into dust   and when a city gives way
to its body   what is it then   what are we
        if we don't see the places we inhabit
            as a living entity   but a machine

I know I am in a body that adheres to form
and structure   but there must be inquiry
beyond the recognition of pattern   I know
there is something here that can't be replicated
        there's no formula for desire
is there   no replication for the honesty of loss
        I'm always afraid that someone will figure this out
that there will be nothing left to understand
        that decisions are less aspirational more outcome based
and beauty   only a contrivance of pleasure

I am afraid that everything becomes abandoned in the end
even the things that make us human

sometimes we get to write the world as we believe it   and therein
is where a mess can begin   the delusion
of certainty   the weaponization of narrative
who would I be if this story wasn't mine to tell
            though   how do I say

I never felt more alive   than when the city was alive
        too   the city can be a living thing can't it
        the streets pulse for me   I swear it

An entire poem precedes the first sentence

      everything begins in an empty field
                 even mercy

          there in the losing
              and what is beyond it

      what beautiful awareness came to me
tightly coiled and spiraled and dense

              my softer heart
      that is home to my rage

The Quiet Room

when the world comes to a still it is a barely noticeable microsecond
what people say is

                        it felt as if my heart stopped

and that is an appropriate metaphor   the life of you stops
for a moment   this is the silent cut   a gentle wounding
that happens over and over again

somewhere else there is someone saying   this is happening
somewhere else   who has become so accustomed to a busy
street or a busy sky that absence is excruciating   imagine our cities in
utter silence   imagine what a sound becomes inside of it   terror is a
life that is constantly upended   everyone sees this   everyone knows
what it looks like now

there are two entirely different places where fear and terror live   one
is imagined   and the other is lived in excruciating detail

You are not complicit in your own destruction   it is fed to you in a
room with no mirrors   a quiet room   where you can't even hear the
sound of your own breath

These things   they move through time   and we act as if nothing can
be done but to ask the next generation to save us from ourselves   I
do not know what it looks like when we win but I'm trying to ask
the question   somewhere inside all of this noise is a proper quiet   I
know this   I can't stop hearing it

it shakes all the comfort out of me

Viable Gods

there are too many gods in the air   capitalism
demands it
          consumable gods   of appreciating value

I got a couple gods in my portfolio just in case
                    only put in as much
          as I was willing to lose   that's what they say
                    you're supposed to do with investments

          this goddamn lens   I'm afraid I'll only ever
see the world within a math of cruel methodologies
          of gods whose actions are always driven by burying intent

that it is always the hand on the plow   but never the garden
          flat and blunt and heavy with premise

what an awful lack of imagination   see what happens when
you grow up in a tract housing development

          what if your god was other people   what if this
was the place
we could house our beliefs   other people can be
terrible   I know
          but so can gods

I am trying to dream better   I really am
          each little blade of grass
                    I'm touching it damnit   I'm touching it

          where is my place without a god   to latch onto
where does one let go   and still remain something

Prayer

what does the earth have to offer you

                                quiet messages

      the slowest possible meter

the field that surrounds you

          aren't you tired of only being a blip in time

refuse this

         everything matters

look at us, always trying to make things small and manageable

         even the world   even time

      what are we when there's nothing left to assign value

they believe everything can be mined for resources

        even the imagined world

      it just takes the right machine

Bioluminescent Worms

Everything changes and nothing changes
that is our precious constant   the way that the body
is the manner of its wanting   if we don't allow for need
this reverent frame can do nothing else but deteriorate
hunger is constant   love is not
                      but desire is
you tell me there are bioluminescent worms
that burrow out once a year from under the sand
somewhere
              you are thinking
                      maybe in the Sahara
but it's likely somewhere less romantic
                   like New Jersey
and every year they emerge   throwing out their seeds
and then die without knowing if anything will come of it
and there is so much sadness
              when you say this
I want to cup your face in my palms because don't all things
desire touch
              and isn't that what a living thing must need
and isn't the worm before dying a desirous creature
one that wishes to be inside the act of living

time is never the same   in all places
          neither as it is on your lips   as it was upon
your neck   that is the strange order of the world
what is it to be a creature that wants
            in all this chaotic redundancy
              isn't it a wondrous thing
to feel the whisper in your stomach

the one

that crawls out of your lips
before you mouth the word   more

This one starts in the middle

the world was slightly less ugly   today   maybe that is enough it's
the constant rupturing   you know   what are we supposed to
do with all of this   I wrote on my dating profile that I am an
agnostic   which is less true these days I do have a god
somewhere   possibly one of cement and asphalt   the
constant whir of a city in motion   when I was 23 I got off
work at this catering job downtown   on my way home I walked
past Grace Jones waiting for her car in front of the hotel   I
may not know my god   yet   but I know what it's like to have
Grace Jones lock eyes on me in front of the Four Seasons   can't
that be a beginning   everyone is writing about the end of the
world and here I am thinking about the start of things like
this morning I woke up   I woke up, again

The Story is the Love Language

I also carry a garden flourishing   here
                where everything changes
      and yet nothing changes   there must be a body
which is also a portal   that brings us
       back to ourselves   I imagine a new word for home
a new place of belonging   one that remains
                       untethered to grief

I only want us to be alive in this world

I only want all the quiet we deserve

I imagine a new word for love
          one that means   here
      I have made for you a space of living
         you   you make me feel material
    we   we will make this world one of brave imagination

stillness is also a weapon   therein

I imagine a new name for the future   what I want
       to offer into this space
      one that says we brought each other back to life
      we did
         we were scared but we did it, anyway

the place of dying should be left only for the older selves
    here   we retain
    our quiet   small is beautiful
                   and the future is

Song

I should have written you a better love poem, it was in me. I held
it through all these nauseous waves of societal collapse. We're
losing every day, and yet I'm here at rest in the possibility of
awakening. Things end, and that is a hurt I'm trying so hard to
not turn away from.

Every song is a love song, it's obsessive— all this bellowing of
demand and regrets— got me listening to this beautifully scaled
vocal run because people can't communicate correctly. I did it all
wrong. Love could have been a more articulate cudgel, but I
chose an artlessness of immense feeling.

In the depths of you I remembered all of me that is soft and
animal and wanting. Your breath which gave me breath, which
gave me breath. Everything in us severed by this country stitched
back together with the barest of thread.

What, if anything, can be sustained these days? Can belonging?
There in time scaling, a bolder me I am still learning to inhabit.
To see a person, to truly see a person, takes a willing focus— to
follow a capture of air down to the bristles of the lungs

into a singular, living heart that endures all that is right and
beautiful in this relentlessly cruel world.

Galactus: Devourer of Worlds

I say yes to this life
full of stop and starts
and all the wrong turns
& the body
made of whiskey
& the body made
of drums
the low hum of 6th & Folsom
in the early morning
praise the creak
of my jawbone
everywhere that hurts on me
is my story
bass in my right knee
bass in my popped calf muscle
and the pitch of my aching back
always my back
I've done things
It ain't always been right
but it got done.
I've eaten this world
plenty
moved from bounce to boogie
sometimes
the earth still shakes at my feet
when the right song comes on
my name
is only what my mouth wants at the time
devourer of worlds

restless sleeper
he who falls
gets up
and falls again.

Mixtape
Les Fleurs, Minnie Riperton (1972)

We have to give ourselves a chance
what flowers in the absence of sight
there is still good root to earth,
to air there alights the enclosure.
In the depths of us, a truer faith
a god of regenerative properties.

for all of these simple things
and much more
a flower was born
it blooms to spread love and joy,
faith and hope
to people forlorn

Who mitigates the looming absence,
a little more time is all, towards what
lays inheritance to the dreaming;
a singular bell, everywhere.
Here, within, the murk and the mud
of us is the unfolding succession
a liberated heart made to tremor
a word that becomes a severance.

for all of these simple things
and much more
a flower was born
it blooms to spread love and joy,
faith and hope
to people forlorn

To seed is to be seeded itself.
In the soil we pray for a new time,
a newer song of revival

Acknowledgments

Thank you Rusty, Laura, and the Omnidawn crew for all the work you've done to bring my work out into the world, and a heartfelt acknowledgement to Ken Keegan.

Gratitude to the editors of the following journals for publishing earlier versions of some of the poems that appear in this book including: Poem-a-Day (May 2023) "Someday, Again", The Offing (May 2024) "The Story is the Love Language", and Diode Editions (September 2024) "Song" and "The Wheel Is."

"In Jerusalem" was originally commissioned for Clarion Alley Mural Project's Wall and Response series.

Some of the poems that appear in this book were repurposed or built off the work I did with Bioneers and their community conversation series as a poetic harvester. Thank you to David Shaw, Nina Simons, and Sharon Zetter for bringing me in to do this work. Extra special thanks to all the participants and speakers I've gotten to partner with in this series including Amisha Ghadiali, Shilpa Jain, Jerry Tello, Clayton Thomas-Muller, Alixa Garcia, Marya Rupa, Kevin John Fong, Zuleikha, Anita Sanchez, Aya De Leon, Jeanine M. Canty, Joan Blades, Nazshonnii Brown-Almaweri, Lauryn D. Smith, Zain Khemani, Mari Margil, Thomas Linzey, and Marilyn Cornelius.

Thank you to Brynn Saito for getting back on that google doc with me to kickstart this whole thing, to Jaz Sufi for helping me through the process of putting this manuscript together, to my Break Room partners, Sam and Hieu, for building our beautiful reading space together, and to every artist, volunteer, and community partner I get to work with at Kearny Street Workshop for inspiring me, for keeping me honest, and grounding my art in community. And thank you to my co-ED at KSW, Mihee Kim. I couldn't have asked for a better partner in this work.

To my family I love you, always. To everyone I love (pets included), you keep me within life.

Jason Bayani is the author of *Locus* (Omnidawn Publishing 2019, Norcal Book Award finalist) and *Amulet* (Write Bloody Publishing 2013). He's an MFA graduate from Saint Mary's College and is the co-executive director of Kearny Street Workshop, the oldest multi-disciplinary Asian Pacific American arts organization in the country. His publishing credits include World Literature Today, Poem-a-Day, Diode Editions, The Offing and other publications. Jason is the recipient of the 2021 California Arts Council Established Artist Fellowship and was a featured artist for the Consortium of Asian American Theaters and Artists Festival in 2022. He performs regularly around the country and debuted his solo theater show "Locus of Control" in 2016 with theatrical runs in San Francisco, New York, and Austin.

Everyone I Love, Alive
by Jason Bayani

Cover design by Kimberley Arteche

Interior design by Laura Joakimson
Interior typefaces: Optima and Joanna MT Std

Printed in the United States
by Books International, Dulles, Virginia
Acid Free Archival Quality Recycled Paper

Publication of this book was made possible in part by gifts from
Katherine & John Gravendyk in honor of Hillary Gravendyk,
Francesca Bell, Mary Mackey, and the New Place Fund

Staff and Volunteers, Fall 2025
Rusty Morrison & Laura Joakimson, co-publishers
Elizabeth Aeschliman, production editor
Sophia Carr, production editor
Rob Hendricks, poetry & fiction editor
Jeffrey Kingman, copy editor
Hazel White, copy editor
Sharon Zetter, poetry editor & book designer
Anthony Cody, poetry editor
Liza Flum, poetry editor
Jennifer Metsker, marketing assistant
Avantika Chitturi, marketing assistant
Angela Liu, marketing assistant